~ 0 ~

TIPS ON HOW TO

REVIVE A FAILING

RELATIONSHIP

TABLE OF CONTENTS

INTRODUCTION

Love is such a beautiful thing, a beautiful sight to behold, one of the best feelings ever and also a great thing to experience. It makes the strongest of hearts weak and weak/hopeless hearts believe in something again. As beautiful and attractive love may sound, it is deadly and can also be the end of a person. It can turn a once sweet world into a bitter place in a very short time. Love is that glue which holds relationships together, regardless of the type of relationship.

This book places its focus on romantic relationships as it is widely the most complex and complicated of all kinds of relationship. A romantic relationship is one in which a person feels very strongly attracted to another person - both to their personality, and most often, physically too. This feeling must also be reciprocated by the other person in order to make the relationship valid. A romantic relationship is that which exists between two people- heterosexual(male and female), homosexual (involving two males or two females) or between more than two people – polyamory. Romantic relationship is the most intimate form of relationship and the parties involved will often describe themselves as being attracted to one another and/or in love. They feel an incredibly strong connection and bond with one another of which they don't share with anyone else, not even a family member which makes it even more special.

Have you been having second thoughts about your partner? Or a two-way feeling, not love but not hate also? Have you been feeling withdrawn from your partner? And after making efforts to change the scenario, it seems to be getting worse? These and many other signs are indicators to a dying relationship. Maybe you are not doing some things right! This book promises to act as a defibrillator in bringing dying relationships back to life.

The book aims at enlightening the parties involved in relationships on how they can revive their lukewarm or seem-to-be-dead relationships and even help spice up happy relationships. It is filled with well explained basics and detailed acts/events that can help turn around the situation of relationships. It will help in understanding the things that should and shouldn't be done in a relationship, things that are being done wrongly and the book will provide practical solutions also, thus, bringing about the needed change in dying romantic relationships.

WHY ARE YOU FALLING OUT OF LOVE?

One unanswered question for everyone in the world is where all those feelings go when we fall out of love. There are many reasons relationship change for the worse but perhaps, the most important things to consider are the problems/difficulties that surround our love and intimacy. The keys to happiness according to a 75-year study by George Vaillant and his team are; 1. *Love and;* 2. *"coping with life in such a way that does not push love away."* Although not easy, it is possible to have a lasting love.

A quote goes thus, "Almost every one of us struggle, to some degree, to stay connected to our loving feelings". Our ability to give and sustain love can be affected by rejections and hurts we might have experienced early on in life. Our defensive shield are being challenged daily by the simple act of giving and sharing love, and this is as a result of the adaptation we have developed along the line of several hurts.

Growing up insecure and with a feeling of neglect has affected a lot of people. They have unintentionally built up defenses and adapted in ways that limit their ability to form a tangible and meaningful connection with someone. This has made a lot of people unknowingly and unintentionally fall out of love many times.

The many differences in upbringing and level of social intelligence has created the fear for love in most people. They feel insecure about love and they whenever they try to share love, this insecurity overshadows them and they fall out of love again and more into this fear of love.

HOW TO DIFFERENTIATE BETWEEN FALLING OUT OF LOVE AND ENTERTAINING FEAR

Despite different beliefs, getting closer to another person tends to increase the fear for intimacy in most people. Therefore, when love happens, we put much effort at first but when it gets more serious or deep, we get scared.

Most times, the real work is not finding the love but rather, the ability to keep being in the love and consistently share it is the hard work. A lot of people nowadays don't realize that they tend to get angry or withdrawn when they experience love to some extent.

Below are some common psychological reasons that make love scare us at times:

I. *Love arouses anxiety and makes us feel vulnerable.*
II. *It brings up sadness and painful feelings from the past (i.e. the lack of love during childhood).*
III. *Love often provokes a painful identity crisis, as we're seen in a new, more positive light.*

IV. *It disconnects people from a "fantasy bond" with their parents or early caretakers.*

V. *It arouses guilt in relation to surpassing a parent or caretaker.*

VI. *Love stirs up painful existential issues and fears around loss.*

SIGNS THAT YOU'RE FALLING OUT OF LOVE

At the point when a relationship turns out to be less essential, there are in many cases a ton of components at play. Dr. John Gottman, one of the main analysts on connections, has endured 25 years noticing couples' communications. He records the four most poisonous ways of behaving between couples, what he calls the "four horsemen," as the accompanying:

Analysis: Would you say you are accusing or going after your partner?

Protectiveness: Would you say you are stopped to input from your partner?

Scorn: Would you say you are feigning exacerbation, ridiculing or driving your partner away?

At the point when we first find love, we will generally treat our partner with a degree of regard and consideration that interfaces with our own caring sentiments. Yet, love isn't simply an inclination that goes back and forth; it comes from this approach to treating one another. We ought to continuously attempt to consider love an action word. It requires genuine activity to exist and flourish. At the point when we participate in horrendous ways of behaving, we give ourselves and our partner a hard nut to crack by restricting articulations/sensations of love. We as a whole, demonstrate in manners we could do without occasionally, however it's generally helpful to consider in the event that any of the four horsemen have walked their direction into any piece of our relationship.

It's additionally useful to consider the accompanying inquiries set out by Dr. Lisa Firestone to assist with assessing what is going on and decide if the actual relationship isn't working.

Is my relationship adversely influencing different parts of my life?

Do I feel resentful and divided a ton of the time?

Am I too diverted by my relationship to work in solid ways?

Do I seldom feel such as myself any longer?

Am I restless or frantic toward my relationship partner?

Do I feel like something is off about me that I am wild to fix?

Has my relationship affected or harmed my friendships?

Has it impacted the manner in which I parent (for example I'm occupied from really focusing on my kids or too dependent on them to address my issues?)

Do I feel constantly embarrassed about myself?

Do I have a down or miserable outlook on my life more often than not?

Assuming that any relationship is causing us this kind of trouble, we might just conclude it isn't appropriate as far as we're concerned. We can cut off the friendship or look for advising that might be useful to us figure out what's happening.

As earlier said, finding the love or falling in love is not the big deal, staying and consistently sharing the love is the hard work. There are several things that leads to falling out of love or that causes failing relationship, most have been mentioned above, now we proffer solutions.

Acknowledging you are falling or you have already fallen out of love is not enough, trying and making sure you revive the failing relationship is the most important step. Knowing you are no longer in love or you are not feeling it as it should be any longer is the first step, the intentional activities to revive the relationship are what follows. These are the things that will be addressed in the consequent chapters.

Find That First Love

Most relationship which ended badly started failing when the first love on which the relationship was built fades off. There are things that must have brought two people together and made them decide to go into a relationship, this or these things can be called "first love". Once it is lost, it becomes hard to go on with the relationship and several issues starts coming up.

In the advent of this kind of situation, searching for that initial trigger, "first love", should be the first step to take in order to savage the relationship. Find that thing you do that makes your partner tick, that thing that makes he or she raves about you and start doing it again. To find this trigger, these steps could be considered:

- Have honest conversation with your partner and discuss what you both have been doing wrong.
- Proffer solutions to the present situation and work towards it.
- Ask each other what you both love about each other and do it more often so as to revive the failing relationship.

- Start making conscious effort to show love to each other. Various ways on showing love are discussed in the consequent chapters.

GET TO KNOW YOUR PARTNER

A lot of relationships nowadays skip the fundamental stage of the relationship which is; 'the getting to know your partner' stage. To have a healthy and lasting relationship, a partner should endeavor to know his or her better-half to the last detail. Knowing your partner can be done in several ways, some examples are listed below:

- **Know their favorites of everything**
  Everybody has something or many things they favor above others, knowing these things help know them better and every partner in a relationship should endeavor to know this things about their partners.
- **Notice every little things; changes in mood, changes in habit, etc.**
  In day to day life, many things happens and it can cause a shift in mood or habit. Noticing these little things in a partner makes them feel valued and loved. It is not necessarily compulsory to find the solution to the mood changes all the time, but noticing it and helping them through it is what is important.

- **Spend time together:**
Spending little or no time with your partner will only distant you from them. The best way to get to know

your partner is by spending more than enough time with them. Go out together, see movies together, have fun together, discuss and argue, these are the things that help you see the perspective of your partner and also help you understand them better. All these can't be achieved if you don't spend time with each other.

- **Exercise together**

Working out or exercising together is another way of getting to know your partner. You get to know their strengths and weakness, their preferences in exercising and how they like to go about it. You also get to get fit together and put each other in check and become healthy both physically and in your relationship.

SHOW LOVE

Everyone desires to be loved and the ability to love your partner well will make a huge a positive impact on your relationship. While you are looking for a new thing to try, use your love for your partner to find ways to communicate that to them, get to know them better, and have a happier and healthier relationship. Find out your partner's love language and how they express it, ask about what makes them feel loved and communicate with them the things you need to feel loved.

Below are few examples of how we can show love:

- **Pick them up from the office during lunch break to dine out together**
  Surprising your partner with a lunch at work or dropping by to eat with them during lunch break is a very nice gesture. It shows you really care about them and you have them in mind always. Having lunch with a love one during break can help blow off some work stress and make a partner happy, thus, making the rest of the working hours productive. It also builds enthusiasm to rush back home to meet their respective partners and continue from where they left off during lunch break. It doesn't have

to be frequent, but it should happen every now and then.

- **Watch your favorite TV show together:**
  Most partners tends to have different favorite TV shows and some knows little or nothing about their partner's favorite show. Trying to know about their favorite shows, why they like it and watching it with them helps to know our partner more and bond while showing love. Doing this will help see things from their perspective, gives you something to talk about aside work and others, gives you a regular bonding time with your partner and helps you know more about your partner.

- **Bring them to a gig or a concert of their favorite band:**
  Music taste differs from one person to another, knowing your partner's taste in music is another love language many overlook. Music can ease stress, reduce anxiety and depression, boost memory and help work out more effectively. Above all, music's effect in a relationship is that it helps partners connect with each other. Knowing your partner's favorite music and band will help you connect with them more, bringing them to a gig of their favorite band will make them appreciate you and increase their live for you.

- **Do not compare your partner**

  People are different, they have different background, different upbringing, different social intelligence level and different ways they express themselves. A mistake lots of couple make is comparing their partner with another person. This demoralizes people and can affect their self-esteem. Once all these starts happening in a relationship, the relationship is heading down the drain. Comparing a partner to another person will only lead to issues here and there and it will affect the health of the relationship. Not comparing your partner is even a love language because it makes them feel at ease and they won't have to be another person with you but themselves.

  Instead of comparing them, do these instead:

  - Be supportive
  - Always see the best in him/her
  - Always show you're lucky to have them.

PLAY AND HAVE FUN

When couples meet at first, they spend significant amount of time engaging in fun activities and spending quality time getting to know each other. But as time goes by, with several additions and changes along the way, such as childbirth, work and so on, the zeal to play or have fun in couples reduces and this in turn takes its toll on the relationship.

It is encouraged that couples find time to play and have fun because, not only is it enjoyable, it can also serve a series of purposes, such as; increase in bonding, communication, conflict resolution and relationship satisfaction, e.t.c.

Below are some play ideas for couples:

> **Take road trips together**: going on road trips is one of the numerous ways of having fun with a partner. You get to see new places together, have a feel of another culture and spend time together and assist each other through the drive. Road trips adds a feel of adventure into a relationship and it can help couples discover hidden aspects of their various partners.

> **Window shop in the mall together**: window shopping is one of the numerous hilarious things of the youth age. Doing it together as a couple

is even better, it gives the avenue for each partner to feel young again. Make a list of your favorite malls and visit them, check out things, play games, try out outfits and take weird pictures, live out a memory you can always revisit during old age. This will help keep the happiness in the relationship as much as the fun in it too.

> **Hike together**: hiking is a really wonderful idea for couples. Especially those who are also concerned about their health and fitness. Hiking in the woods or mountains with a lot of history is a life saver. Asides from the incredible nature around you while hiking, it allows couple to know the fear of their partners and help them move on from it, without cutting out the fun of adventure.

> **Plan a picnic at the park:** Picnics are great ways to bond with a partner. It gives time and space to discuss intimately in a natural setting. Having several picnics at different parks or even just a park, making it a favorite spot helps a relationship grow and remain strong.

While planning a picnic, here are some things to put in place for a memorable one:

- Prepare snacks to eat while talking
- Pack some drinks
- Make some desserts
- Avoid messy foods.

➢ **Plan a trip to the museum**: museums are historical places and contrary to most thinking that it is a boring place, it is actually a great place to visit with a partner. It encourages laughter and awesome conversation and it's a place to explore and learn new things.
Museums are reasonable destination for couples due to the following:

- You always have things to talk about.
- They are affordable
- They are filled with memories of the past, creating a new memory in that setting is a nice thing.

➢ **Book tickets for you two for the premiere of their favorite movie**: watching movie is a fun escape from reality. Watching a movie together and having discussion about it is another avenue for bonding in relationship. To make it more romantic, getting tickets for the premiere of a partner's favorite movie is a very nice way of showing love and it makes them happy. Going together, spending time together and having a laugh together in the cinema is a bonding memory and the stronger the bonds between partners, the better the relationship.

➢ **Do groceries shopping together**: Groceries are one of the daily needs of every human. Food is a very important aspect of life and shopping for the food together or other necessary needs for the household helps put partners on the same page. It also affords them the opportunity to do other things like:

- Plan their week ahead
- Time to plan a special meal
- Talk budget
- Reminds them how well they work together
- Can be substituted as a small date

DEVELOP TOGETHER

For any relationship to last long, both partners must endeavor to grow. Having that in mind, they should grow together so as to bring oneness and not make either party feel left out in the relationship.

This chapter will point out several ways in which partners can work on themselves together and grow together.

- **Plan your future together—make a vision board**: Most of the broken relationships nowadays starts breaking when the one party starts achieving his or her life goals. This usually occur because most times, each partner makes goals or set targets without considering a second party right from start. Thus, making it hard to reach some needed compromises for the relationship to work.

  To curtail this common situation, planning a future together with respective partner is one of the best way if not the best way to go about it. Planning together helps brings about the following in a relationship:
  - Gain clarity as a couple

- Deepens connection amongst partners
- Accountability, cheerleading and action

How do we create a vision board?
- **Take it slow**: rushing into anything has never being the right way to go about anything in life and this applies to this to. To create a working vision board with a partner, find time to first share what your various goals are, discuss extensively and agree on what to start with, include or pend for the time being.
- **Create categories**: A good structure is very good in life and dividing your vision board to various categories will make it easier to work on and really achieve it. Categories can include: family, finances, career/business, health and fitness, travel and leisure, education and hobbies, spirituality, assets.
  There can be more or less in a vision board but having categories helps make realization easy.
- **Set a timeframe**: Most couple falls off along the road when it comes to making the visions a reality and this is mostly because there is a lack of timeframe for the vision. As you are making the vision board, set a timeframe – a reasonable one

at that. This will help you know when you are getting complacent or nonchalant.

While creating a vision board, we have to be very careful not to be suffocating the other partner unintentionally. The following steps can help achieve that:

- Don't try to be too controlling.
- Lead by example instead of constant nagging about a target.
- Be open to your partner and be flexible in your decisions.

- **Learn something new together**: Bonding over learning is something couples should try out. Learning can be fun when it includes a partner, it creates an avenue for discussions, fun argument, practicing together, helping each other out when the going gets tough and it also helps in the growth of each partners. Things couples could learn together includes:

  Languages
  - how to cook a romantic meal
  - how to play an instrument'
  - self-defense moves
  - yoga moves
  - how to give CPR
  - history behind cities
  - The secret things that turns you on.

➤ **Serve or volunteer together**: Volunteering has been discovered to keep couples together. It even brought about a saying that;

>"couples who volunteer together, stays together".

Volunteer helps people develop selfless skills and brings you close to people around you. Imagine having that with your partner, you both develop more social skills, your Emotional Quotient increases, you get to see the community around you and doing all this together will reflect positively in the relationship.

Couples who volunteer have been found to have a great sense of gratitude and happiness because they appreciate the good things they share in life together and it also gives them a sense of purpose outside relationship settings.

➤ **Read a book together and have your little1:1 book club**: Reading is a powerful tool in self-development. Reading allows the mind to travel far and imagine things freely without limits, doing this with a lover is very enjoyable. Here are few things reading together with a partner does;

- They discover new things together
- They are happier and smarter
- They find each other more attractive than before.
- They enjoy each other's company

- They can discover innate things about each other.
- They enjoy healthy connections
- They find it easy to keep a conversation with other.

➢ **Learn to play different instruments and play songs together**: Playing instrument is the beginning of a journey and even though it is challenging it has a lot of benefits and sharing the benefits with a love one is really wonderful. These are some of the effects of playing an instrument:

- Reduces stress
- Produces patience and perseverance
- Cultivates creativity
- Allows you to share with others
- Increases personal discipline

➢ **Challenge one another and set a time limit**: Engaging in couple challenges and making videos is another way of having fun and creating memories which can always be re-visited. In these challenges, a couple has to do an activity or a task together within a stipulated time to call it a win. To add to the fun, doing the challenges with several couples is a great feeling. Examples of challenges for couples to do:

- Smell and guess

- Staring contest
- Guess the movie
- Karaoke time
- Guess the line
- Complete the sentence
- Role-play.

Conclusion

Relationships are full of ups and downs. Things can't be a bed of rose all the time, there will always be challenges but the ability to stand right up and bounce back each time makes it easier for relationships to come back to life rather than the parties involved choosing to stay at the rock bottom.

It is assumed that by the time the reader gets to this point of the piece, lots of lesson must have been learnt and new ideas of mending broken relationships must have been gained as well.